AF191116

EioS
Anxiety ? Away with it

Michael Barten-Renon

Anxiety? Away with it!

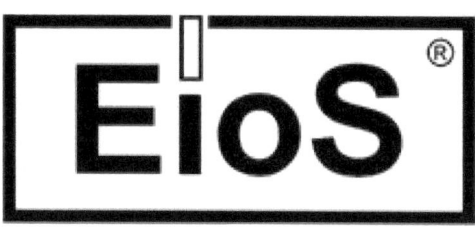

A self-help book for those with anxiety and stress

Michael Barten-Renon

Bibliographic information from the Deutsche Nationalbibliothek: The Deutsche Nationalbibliothek lists this publication in the Deutsche Nationalbibliografie; detailed bibliographic data is available on the Internet at dnb.dnb.de.

Production and publishing:
BoD – Books on Demand, Norderstedt

CONTENTS

About the author

Michael Barten-Renon developed
EioS therapy in the year 2009. He was the first
person to succeed in separating stressful
emotions from their causes in the long term by
using a set script to stimulate states in the
brain, thereby interrupting the supply to the
neuronal structure in question.

Causes and their effects are deleted without
affecting the memory. This enables those
affected to relearn the experiences, events and
situations.

Michael Barten-Renon thus refutes the
conventional medical opinion that feelings
CANNOT be treated directly.
Michael Barten-Renon would like to make this
script available to everyone worldwide in the
form of this book, so that people can free
themselves from fears and burdens.

This project was realised with the support of his
long-time friend Andreas Sauter.

Michael Barten-Renon has trained over 150 doctors, psychologists and educators since 2013 and, with over 2,000 treatments and 500 new patients every year, is one of the most popular psychotherapeutic practitioners in the world. In his field, he is recognised as an absolute expert in the areas of panic attacks, anxiety and stress disorders and psychogenic illnesses.

Michael Barten-Renon began implementing the digitalisation of EioS therapy in 2014. This is how the world's first fully automated, interactive, psychotherapeutic app was created, which was released in 2022 after 8 years of development and currently has 58 application areas in 6 languages. The EioS app is authorised as a medical device throughout Europe. On the next page you will find a barcode that makes it easier to access the EioS app.

EioS app: The digital option for self-treatment

In addition to our book, we offer you the opportunity to use our EioS app with over 50 application areas to treat different, specific anxiety and stress disorders. The EioS app is the world's first fully automated, interactive app for the treatment of psychogenic disorders.
It is authorised as a medical device throughout Europe and is currently available in six different languages: German, English, French, Spanish, Russian and Turkish.

A male or female voice is available for each of these languages. The development team is constantly working on expanding our treatment portfolio and implementing additional languages.

Try out the EioS app now!

Training programmes and self-study courses

For several years, EioS Therapiezentren GmbH has been offering psychologists, doctors and alternative practitioners for psychotherapy training to become certified EioS therapists. While this could previously only be completed in the form of face-to-face seminars, the courses will also be offered online as self-study courses in future. In addition, we are now expanding our training programme for those without a therapeutic background, which deals in more detail with areas of application, troubleshooting, and the basics of EioS Therapy.

You can find more information here:

ausbildung.eiostherapie.de

The basics of EioS therapy

Would you like to find out more about EioS therapy?

In **"How does EioS work?"** we show you:

1. how the limbic system works
2. how mental illnesses arise from biographical events
3. the medical and psychological principles of EioS therapy
4. how EioS dissolves negative life structures

Click here to go directly to the video:

You can find more information on our website:

www.eiostherapie.de

Introduction

Dear readers and sufferers
The worst danger to our health is fear. It not only burdens our psyche, but also our body by weakening our immune system and making it ill.
Many illnesses are of our own making.
They are caused by constant stress and strain as a result of anxiety and unprocessed experiences.

This book is designed to help people treat themselves for anxiety, phobias and emotional conflicts, and improve their quality of life. It serves as a home medicine chest for the psyche and is intended to enable people to alleviate or even resolve symptoms of anxiety, phobias and stress in themselves or others.

This book is available in 15 languages in 39 countries and encapsulates the treatment process of EioS therapy in a simple form for self-treatment of acute anxiety and stress. It is based on the experience of over 80,000 treatments with EioS therapy.
The central focus of this form of therapy is the direct treatment

of emotions in panic attacks, specific fears, phobias, post-traumatic stress, compulsions and psychosomatic illnesses.
The content of this book is a partial extract of the daily therapy process as it is applied in our practices.

So if you follow the instructions in this book, you can succeed in decoupling stressful emotions from the cause in 14 steps and successfully & sustainably dispel the symptom.

These emotions include

Fears of objects, fears of situations, fears of people, fears of myths, panic attacks, fear of loss, fear of separation, fear of illness, fear of death, existential fears, suffering, pain, grief, jealousy, offence, humiliation, anger, hatred, helplessness, powerlessness, disappointment, contempt, aversion, disgust, shame, torment, longing and other feelings.

The effect may be limited or unsuccessful in the following circumstances:

a) lack of suffering

b) conscious or unconscious morbid gain

c) limited mental capacity

d) psychoses

e) behavioural and personality disorders

f) utilisation of psychotropic substances

g) organic brain damage

h) organic influences on the psyche

The book is designed so that you can carry out this process on others or yourself completely safely. Simply follow the instructions and stick to the process. You can't go wrong with this.

The contents of this book do not lead to contraindications or side effects and can be used with children and people of advanced age.
It serves to alleviate acute anxiety and stress, but is no substitute for a doctor or therapist.

"Every unprocessed event makes us ill. It has an effect on the organism, even when we don't think about it."

Michael Barten-Renon
Fondateur de la Thérapie EioS

Anxiety? Away with it!

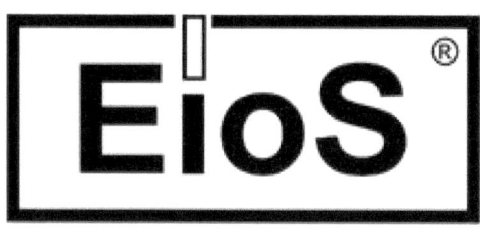

Part 1 : Self-treatment

Michael Barten-Renon

Instructions for self-treatment

1. Find a place where you are undisturbed. Sit or lie down and start reading the first step, in which you are asked to imagine the topic you want to cover. Only when this topic evokes a feeling or emotion (physical reaction) are you ready to treat yourself.

2. Always close your eyes when you are asked to do so and only open your eyes again when you have reached the goal of the respective step. **Each page corresponds to one step.**

3. Before you close your eyes, you must be aware of the text you have read for each step.

4. If you experience any difficulties with your imagination during the treatment process, you can rest assured, because the quality of your imagination is not so important for the effect. In this case, you just have to pretend that it is.

5. If emotions intensify during self-treatment, you should continue the process with determination, as you will benefit from it. During the actions to be carried out, the emotions are reduced and the pressure of suffering eases.

6. If the process is interrupted, repeat the last step and continue the treatment. If the treatment cannot be carried out on the same day, start the next day with Step 1.

7. Sentence positions given in the therapy process are not subject to grammatical order, but have a therapeutic purpose.

Step 1

Realise now why you are undergoing this treatment. Think about what is bothering you or scaring you. You will now feel a physical reaction that is noticeable either in your head, throat, chest or stomach.

This emotion becomes a little clearer when you close your eyes and breathe out completely. When you can clearly feel this sensation in one or more places, open your eyes again.

Step 2

You now feel discomfort in one or more places. In the following step, imagine that you reach with both hands into your head, neck, chest or stomach, depending on where you feel it most clearly, and grasp this feeling with both hands as if you were holding a ball. To do this, close your eyes and only open them again when you have the ball safely in your hands.

Step 3

Now carefully lift this feeling out to the front and place it in your lap. If you still feel something in that place, repeat the process until it feels empty or neutral.

To do this, close your eyes and only open them when you can **no** longer feel **anything** in that area of your body.

Step 4

Now check whether you still perceive emotions in the other three areas of your body when you think about the cause of your problem. If you no longer feel anything in your head, neck, chest or stomach, *step 3* is complete. However, if you can still feel something in other areas, repeat *step 3* until you can **no** longer feel **anything** in your head, neck, chest or stomach.

*If you feel emotions on your arms or legs, wipe them down with your hands until you can **no** longer feel anything there either. The stripped off material should then also be placed on the lap.*

Step 5

Now you should not feel anything in any area of the body when you think of the cause or the trigger. Now imagine that there is a plastic bag with a zip to your right. It does not matter whether it is round or square. Imagine opening this zip and stuffing all your feelings from your lap into this bag. The bag is stretchy and everything will fit inside. Close your eyes now and only open them when you have packed everything into the bag and closed the zip.

Step 6

You don't need to close your eyes for this step.
Now take the bag under your arm, go into your bathroom and hold the bag over the sink.
Now lift it up a little and you will see a valve on the underside of the bag. This may have a colour in your imagination. Just memorise it.
Now open this valve and a broth begins to run out of the bag.
This broth may also have a colour that you can remember. If the broth smells in your imagination, this is not unusual.

Step 7

Now turn on the cold water so that it no longer smells that way and so that the broth can drain better. You can now see the broth running out of the bag and feel that you are getting more and more comfortable as the bag empties.

To do this, close your eyes and only open them when the bag is completely empty.

Step 8

The bag is now empty and it is now necessary to remove the valve from the bag. Rinse it under cold water and then place it on the edge of the sink.
Then turn off the cold water and, if available, remove the plug from the drain and stuff the bag and zip into the drain. Don't worry, nothing will get blocked. Now close your eyes and only open them again when the bag and zip are completely stuffed in.

Step 9

Now turn on the hot water so that the bag and zip can dissolve. Hot water dissolves the bag and the zip fastener like sugar or gelatine. While the bag and zip are dissolving, wipe out the sink with both hands to make it nice and clean. The washbasin becomes nice and clean, nice and clean. Because the washbasin symbolises your soul. By wiping out the sink, you cleanse your soul of all the burdens, emotional conflicts and fears that have led you to this treatment. Close your eyes now and only open them again when the sink is nice and clean.

Step 10

Now the sink is nice and clean, nice and clean, nice and clean.

Now take the valve from the edge of the sink in both hands and start rolling it into a ball. Just as you can shape dough or plasticine into a ball, you can shape this valve into a ball by rolling it. And the longer you roll this ball, the smaller and harder it becomes. Close your eyes now and only open them when the ball has become as big as a glass marble and as hard.

Step 11

Now put the ball back on the edge of the sink, go outside your house and look up at the sky. You see a beautiful blue sky and a single small, white cloud. It will open in a moment and a ray of light will come out. It is healing, bright light. Now stand in the cone of light so that you can feel the warmth of this light.

Now close your eyes briefly until you can feel the warmth and only then continue reading on **the next page**.

Continue reading on the next page

Step 11

This light will now fill the places in your body where all the stressful feelings and emotions have been.

Your burdens, emotional conflicts and fears are now completely extinguished and you can live your life free from them.

Every thought and every reminder of the causes of your symptoms will no longer trigger any emotional reactions.

Take as much of this light as you can get.
The cloud only closes when every single cell in your body is filled.

Before you close your eyes, think about the **last five sentences** again. You only open them when every single cell in your body is full and the symptom-free parts of your body are full and closed.

Step 12

Now go back into the house, into the bathroom and stand in front of the ball. You look at the ball, read the following lines **aloud** and become **aware** of their meaning.

Dear little glass ball,

I am very grateful that you were with me.

You were very important to me.

There will never be room for you again where you have lived until now,

because that is where the healing, bright light is now.

I am very grateful that you were with me.

Everything I have said and imagined is true and deeply anchored in my subconscious.

Continue reading on the next page

Step 12

Deep in my subconscious is anchored the knowledge that a healing bright light dwells in the places where the stressful feelings and emotions once prevailed.

This light will ensure that I can live without these burdens or fears in the future.

Every thought and every memory of what caused it will not evoke any distressing emotions and feelings.

Everything I have said and imagined today is true and deeply anchored in my subconscious.

Step 13

Now imagine that you take a hairbrush and smash the ball with the back of the brush. Keep beating until the shards and the powder are very fine. The finer they become, the lighter they become.

Close your eyes now and only open them when the powder is white.

Step 14

Now clean up the brush again and sweep the powder from the edge of the sink into the basin by hand and turn on the cold water. Now rinse the sink and your hands free of the powder and then turn the water off again.
Then lie down for a while, close your eyes and rest.

Anxiety? Away with it!

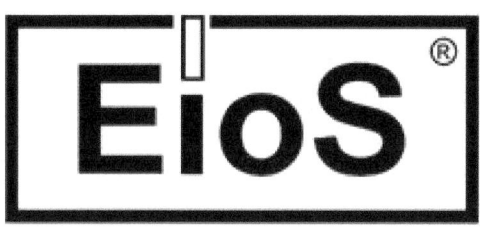

Partie 2 : Treatment of others

Michael Barten-Renon

Guidance on the treatment of others

1. Find a place where you can both be undisturbed. Sit down together and briefly discuss the topic. Then start reading the first step.

2. Every single page is a step. The text is to be reproduced exactly as it is written. Then wait for the answer or reaction.

3. If difficulties with the imagination arise during the treatment process, the patient can be reassured that the quality of the imagination does not play such an important role. In this case, the patient only has to pretend that it is so.

4. If emotions become stronger during the process, e.g. if the person concerned begins to cry excessively when dealing with the issues of grief or fear, the application should be continued imperatively. During the actions to be carried out, the emotions are reduced and the pressure of suffering eases.

5. The process can be
   and continued at a later time (within
   one hour).

6. All texts in a normal font (not in italics)
   are read aloud to the person being
   treated. Texts in italics are annotations
   only.

7. The following script talks about fears
   and stresses. If you know the topic you
   are dealing with, you can replace the
   words "fear", "anxiety" and "stress" with
   words relevant to your own topic.
   Example: Your counterpart is afraid of
   flying. Instead of "Now close your eyes
   and think about what is scaring or
   stressing you", say: "Now close your
   eyes and think about your fear of flying
   and how you will board an aeroplane
   next time."

8. Sentence positions given in the therapy
   process are not subject to grammatical
   order, but have a therapeutic purpose.

Step 1

Now close your eyes and think about what scares you or burdens you.

(Give the person a few seconds to empathise with the situation.)

The feeling you associate with it, where do you feel it most clearly?
In your head,
in your throat,
in your chest or
in your stomach?
(Wait for answer)

Step 2

If you could reach into the body with your hands and grab the feeling and just lift it out, would you need one or both hands?
(Wait for answer)

Now imagine that you are gripping your body with both hands, grasping the feeling on the left and right as if you were holding a ball. When you have it safely in your hands, let me know.
(Wait for answer)

Step 3

Now wiggle, jiggle and shake this feeling until it feels loose, then carefully lift it out to the front and place it in your lap. Repeat this process until the area feels empty or neutral. Let me know when you are finished.

(If the person concerned has difficulty imagining this, he or she should pretend that it is the case. The effect is the same.)

Step 4

Do you feel the fear or the stressful feeling in another place?
If no -
continue with Step 5.
If yes -
Where do you still feel it?
(Wait for answer)

Then reach in there with both hands, grab the feeling on the left and right, wiggle, shake and shake it until it is loose and carefully lift it out to the front and place it in your lap. Repeat this process until you can **no** longer feel **anything**. When you are finished, let me know.

Step 4 must be repeated until the question "Do you still feel the fear or the stressful feeling in another place?" is answered with **NO**.

Step 5

I want you to imagine that there is a plastic bag with a zip to your right. Is the bag round or square in your imagination?
(Wait for answer. The form has no relevance)

Now open the zip and put all the feelings from your lap into the bag.
Don't worry, everything fits into the bag, it stretches. Let me know when you've finished.

Step 6

You close the bag, put it under your arm and go into your bathroom. Hold the bag over the sink, lift it up a little and you will see a valve at the bottom of the bag. What colour is the valve?
(Wait for answer. The colour has no relevance)

Now open the valve and a broth begins to run out. What colour is the broth?
(Wait for answer. The colour has no relevance)

Now switch on the cold water so that the broth can drain better. And the broth runs and runs and runs, and the more that runs out of the bag, the more comfortable you feel. It's only coming in bursts and if it starts to drip, let me know.

Step 7

Now the bag is empty, remove the valve from the bag, rinse it under cold water and then place it on the edge of the sink.

Let me know when you are finished.

Step 8

Now turn off the cold water, remove the plug from the drain and stuff the bag and zip into the drain. Don't worry, nothing will get blocked.

Let me know when you are finished.

Step 9

Now turn on the hot water so that the bag can dissolve.
Hot water dissolves the bag and the zip fastener like sugar or gelatine.
While the bag is dissolving, wipe out the sink with both hands to make it nice and clean.
The washbasin becomes nice and clean, nice and clean.
This is because the washbasin symbolises your soul, and your soul is now being washed clean of all its fears and burdens.
And when the sink is nice and clean, you let me know.

Step 10

Now you can turn off the
hot water. Then put the stopper back into
the spout, take the valve in both hands and
start rolling it into a ball.
Just as you can mould dough or plasticine
into a ball, you can mould this valve into a
ball. And the longer you roll this ball, the
smaller and harder it becomes.

And when the ball is as big as a glass
marble and as hard, let me know.

Step 11

Now take the ball and place it back on the edge of the sink. Then you go out of the house into the open air and look up at the sky.

You see a beautiful blue sky and a single, small white cloud in the sky. And this cloud breaks in the centre, it opens slowly and a ray of light comes out. It is healing, bright light. This light will now fill and close the places where your fears and burdens have been residing. It will ensure that you never have to experience these stressful feelings again. You will now be able to live without suffering.

Take as much of this light as you can get. The cloud only closes when every single cell in your body is filled and all the holes are closed and healed.

Let me know when the cloud closes.

(Wait for answer. May take longer at this point)

Step 12

Now go back into the bathroom and stand in front of the
ball and repeat the following after me:
*(The person being treated must
repeat every single line out loud)*

Dear little glass ball,

I am very grateful that you were with me.

You were very important to me.

There will never be room for you again where you have lived until now,

because that is where the healing, bright light is now.

I am very grateful that you were with me,

you were very important to me.

Step 13

Now take a hairbrush and
smash the crystal ball with the back of the
brush. You keep hitting it
until the shards are reduced to
powder. The finer the powder becomes, the
brighter it gets. When the powder is white,
you indicate this.

It is now permitted to ask how you
feel now. The symptom should
be alleviated or disappear completely.
This process can be repeated after three days at
the earliest.

Step 14

Now use your hand to sweep the
powder into the sink and
switch on the cold water in order to wash
the

powder away from the sink and your hands.
Then turn off the water again.

Then lie down for a while, close
your eyes and rest.